I0224279

Reuniting the Children of Abraham

The Sacred Story that Calls Jews,
Christians and Muslims to Peace

Brenda Naomi Rosenberg

To learn more about this book and its author, please visit
www.BrendaNaomiRosenberg.com

Copyright © 2020 by Brenda Naomi Rosenberg
All Rights Reserved

Abraham's Tears lyrics reprinted with permission of Edna
Garte, Harbor Wind Music, Waterford, Michigan.

ISBN: 978-1-64180-071-6
Version 1.0

Cover design and illustration by Rick Nease
www.RickNeaseArt.com

Published by
Front Edge Publishing
42807 Ford Road, Suite 234
Canton, Michigan

Front Edge Publishing books are available for discount
bulk purchases for events, corporate use and small groups.
Special editions, including books with corporate logos,
personalized covers and customized interiors are available
for purchase. For more information, contact Front Edge
Publishing at info@FrontEdgePublishing.com.

This book is dedicated to all the children of Abraham:

Descendants as beautiful and numerous as the stars in
the sky, each one of us a world unto ourselves,
yet by joining together we are magnificent and limitless as
the heavens, a luminescent galaxy of stars
that can light the way to peace.

Praise for
Reuniting the
Children of Abraham

This project is a powerful experience that gives hope to the idea of these three religions being able to find their common heritage as a reason for mutual religious respect and spiritual healing in the future.

Producer John P. Blessington, CBS Entertainment

Once we rediscover our shared origin story in the ancient family of Abraham—Jews, Christians and Muslims living today must face the powerful truth that God still is calling us to reunite our family.

David Crumm, Detroit Free Press

In her resolve to reconnect the Children of Abraham, Brenda Naomi Rosenberg recognizes that tension has eroded our shared traditions deeply rooted in our Abrahamic ancestry. Yet by harnessing the the tension that once separated us, Brenda and I now share an unshakable bond, rooted not only in our commonalities but also in our differences.

Samia Moustapha Bahsoun, co-author of *Harnessing the Power of Tension*

We all want people to be able to experience religious diversity and not be afraid of the differences that seem so new to them, at first. Our Girl Scout Law is rooted in the commitment to make the world a better place. Our girls come from every religious tradition. Whatever their individual background may be, we want our girls to see that their ideas, hopes and dreams can contribute to peace in our community and the world.

Suzanne Bante, chair of Religious Relationships Committee, Girl Scouts of Southeastern Michigan

Brenda Rosenberg's targets have been prejudice, misconception, fear and hatred. Rising global anti-Semitism and anti-Zionism have fueled her cause, but so has a relentless desire to forge partnerships from seeming stone—and to spur understanding despite the divides.

Robert Sklar, The Detroit Jewish News

Foreword

Some years ago, I created a birthday present for my dear friend Brenda. It was a clear plastic replica of a Nobel Peace Prize, engraved with her name. I meant it as a place holder for the actual prize I'm convinced she'll receive someday. If it doesn't materialize, that's okay, too. Because Brenda knows how hard she's tried. Because ever since 9/11, my friend has worked tirelessly to nurture relations between groups and individuals who feel estranged from each other.

I've been awestruck by Brenda's resilience and determination. I was with her once when a man came up and spat at her, accusing her of naiveté and selling out. Such hostility would have had me running for the door. Brenda replied graciously to her accuser. After, I expressed amazement at her calm. "Oh, I've had much worse," she said, laughing it off.

Some 20 years ago, Brenda and I attended a program by Debbie Ford, whose book *The Dark Side of the Light Chasers* helped both of us through difficult times. My response, as a lifetime journalist, was to write my first memoir, *Back from Betrayal: Saving A Marriage, A Family, A Life*. Brenda's response was to create a program of her own, drawing perceived enemies or people with opposing views together in a safe space to share thoughts and fears about "the other." Her approach fosters understanding and reduces fear. Participants realize how much they have in common.

Some years ago, Brenda created Reuniting the Children of Abraham. The program is a brave and insightful way of breaking down stereotypes and cracking through our shells to the soft, inner core we share. RTCOA participants remain true to themselves and their beliefs while still honoring those of their perceived enemies. Participants come away with an intact sense of dignity and self-respect.

Reuniting the Children of Abraham accomplishes the seemingly impossible feat of bringing Christians, Muslims and Jews together through their common ancestry. The program has accomplished many breakthroughs, brought many strangers together. This book about the program is a goldmine of inspiring stories, stories that unlock deeply felt, seldom shared emotions. A book that will change how you see the world.

Brenda never had biological children of her own. Instead, she has dozens of spiritual children, girls and boys she's inspired. And lately dozens more—Catholic Girl Scouts whom she's embraced, inspired, educated and taught to bake challah bread.

I'm a story teller. I've been telling and sharing stories for over 50 years, as a journalist, author and columnist. I've been telling Brenda's story for most of my career, early on as a fashion and design editor. I accompanied her to New York and marveled at the relationships she built with designers such as Oscar de la Renta and Calvin Klein, at the ultra-chic high heels she insisted on wearing to their studios. Brenda was my go-to resource for the latest fashion trends.

Telling stories is how we preserve and understand our lives. How we establish and preserve our legacy. I want my grandchildren to know how I see and experience the world. I write about joys and sorrows and how I cope.

Telling stories is how all of us will be remembered. How we want to be remembered. As hard as we work to discourage it, however many doctors we visit and vitamins we take, we all pay the ultimate price for the inestimable gift of life. Even if we have the character of an Abraham Lincoln or a Mahatma Gandhi. If we're lucky, we'll live on through our descendants. Not only through our DNA, but through the wisdom we've imparted. Through the stories we tell them about us, the stories they pass on.

Brenda and the friends who helped her create RTCOA hope the stories in this book will inspire parents and mentors to nurture compassionate, caring children. Compassionate, caring children grow into compassionate, caring adults, citizens and peace makers.

According to scripture in all the great religions, to save one life is to save the world. Readers of this book will be inspired by an unlikely champion, a Jewish fashionista who is doing her part to change the world. Reading this book might just inspire you to do the same.

As Brenda says on her cellphone answering machine: Shalom. Salaam. Peace.

—Suzy Farbman

Suzy Farbman is a veteran journalist and author of the memoir, *GodSigns: Health, Hope and Miracles, My Journey to Recovery.* She has promoted interfaith peacemaking with Brenda Naomi Rosenberg over many years.

How do we
greet each other
in peace?

Jews say: "Shalom aleichem," which means
"Peace be upon you."
(Read more:
https://en.wikipedia.org/wiki/Shalom_aleichem)

Muslims say: "As salamu alaykum," which means
"Peace be upon you."

The Muslim response to this greeting is: "Wa alaykumu
salam," which means "And peace be upon you, too."
(https://en.wikipedia.org/wiki/As-salamu_alaykum)

Christians say: "Peace be with you."

The Christian response to this greeting is:
"And also with you."

Abraham's Tears

A song by Edna Garte

By the banks of the Jordan, a man long in years
Watching the river said, "These are my tears
These are my children, caught in the mud
That turns wisdom to sorrow and wine into blood"

I stopped as I saw him, his beard white with age
He looked like he'd stepped out of history's page
He said, "I can see you would ask you I am
Since I had one vision, I'm called Abraham

"And these are my children, I once watched in play
They splashed in this river in the light of the day
These are my children, who tell of my life
I wish I could hold them, and heal all their strife"

By the bands of the Jordan I held him again
My old, long-lost father, my old long-lost friend
He showed me a paper that loosely was rolled
And this song that I'm singing is the story it told"

He cried, "Oh my children, please come back to me
For now in each other, my face you can see"
He cried, "Oh my children, your grief is my own
Your tears are my warning, your love is my home

"These are my children, and they are my life,
And this is God's country, when free from their strife"

How can Abraham be a symbol of unity today?

Abraham continues to call people together as he did at the time of his death. The Bible says that his long-separated sons Isaac and Ishmael returned to bury their father.

> *"This is the length of Abraham's life: 175 years.*
>
> *Abraham breathed his last and died in a good old age, an old man and full of years, and was gathered to his people.*
>
> *His sons Isaac and Ishmael buried him in the cave of Machpelah.*
>
> *There Abraham was buried, with his wife Sarah."*
>
> **Genesis 25:7-10**

> *"Abraham's death promotes peace. At Abraham's burial, his two most prominent sons, rivals since before they were born, estranged since childhood, scions of rival nations, come together for the first time since they were rent apart nearly three-quarters of a century earlier. The text reports their union without comment— but the meaning of this moment cannot be diminished. Abraham achieves in death what he could never achieve in life: a moment of reconciliation between his two sons, a peaceful, communal, side-by-side flicker of possibility in which they are not rivals, scions, warriors, adversaries, children, Jews, Christians or Muslims. They are brothers."*
>
> **From Bruce Feiler's Abraham: A Journey to the Heart of Three Faiths**

What is Reuniting the Children of Abraham?

Reuniting the Children of Abraham is a powerful peace initiative that was launched in 2004. Drawing on the creative arts of drama, music, improvisation and interactive dialogue, this is a model partnership that was created to build bridges of understanding between Christians, Muslims and Jews.

This story of hope and resilience began with a tiny spark. Sometimes tiny sparks trigger bombs. In this case, the spark lit candles in the darkness.

As news stories about conflict and terrorism continue to explode around the world, consider for a moment this very different kind of story. It's about a Muslim cleric who shared the spark of an idea with a Jewish friend over coffee—an idea that sparked her dreams. Then, Brenda Naomi Rosenberg used that initial spark to kindle the creative energies of teenagers, religious leaders, theater professionals and university scholars. Before long, Brenda's dream had turned to reality. Since that time, her ideas have changed countless lives, fueled theatrical productions, fostered the development of interfaith organizations and led to coverage on network TV. In 2020, that initial spark helped to launch an innovative cross-cultural project among Girl Scouts in southeast Michigan to foster a new generation of peacemakers.

Here is founder Brenda Naomi Rosenberg's story:

After the terrorist attacks on Sept 11, 2001, I dedicated myself to building bridges of understanding between southeast Michigan's diverse communities. On a fall afternoon in 2002, Sharona Shapiro, director of the Michigan American Jewish Committee, and I hosted a lunch for Rabbi David Rosen from Jerusalem to meet some of Michigan's Muslim community leaders.

That day, Detroit Imam Abdullah El Amin and I lingered over coffee, wanting to speak further about our concerns for the rise in hatred, terrorism and global conflict. We both felt there had to be steps we could take to help to ease global tensions.

Sipping my coffee, I asked the Imam, "What would create better understanding between your Muslim community, my Jewish community and Christian communities?"

He paused for a moment, then said, "If we would only remember that we share the same father, Father Abraham, we might find ways to bring our family back together again."

El Amin pointed to a passage in the Bible in which Abraham's long-separated sons, Ishmael and Isaac, came together at Abraham's death to bury their father.

Then, El Amin said to me: "We're tearing our world apart today. Why can't we do what Ishmael and Isaac did and come back together as family?"

As we left our table, my heart was filled with both sadness and a renewed hope.

That night, I dreamt about a theater stage. On it, Isaac and Ishmael left the caves of Machpelah together. As they started to turn away from each other, Archangel Raphaela flew into this scene and wrapped her wings around the grieving brothers, asking them to sit down. Then, she guided them through a four-step healing process of reconciliation:

Step 1: *Break bread together.*

Step 2: *Listen with compassion. Tell their stories of what it was like to be Abraham's son.*

Step 3: *Be the other. Step into the other's shoes and retell the story from the other's point of view.*

Step 4: *Create something new together.*

In my dream, the brothers agreed to write a play for young people on how compassionate listening can lead to understanding each other's positions and begin the reconciliation process. They also decided to include stories from teens who had undergone shifts in attitude and learned how to break the cycles of fear, hate and intolerance.

The next morning, I telephoned Imam El Amin and the Rev. Dan Buttry, who was then the head of global reconciliation programs for the Baptist Peace Fellowship. We met two days later to share lunch and read from the texts of the Torah, New Testament and Quran. By late afternoon we had created an outline for a project that would engage teens in both the creation of a new play and in a new kind of dialogue that would extend from the play into the future.

Soon after, I explained our concept to my friends Julie Cummings and Victor Begg. Julie suggested I call Rick Sperling at Mosaic Youth Theatre. Victor Begg, who was then the chair of National Conference for Community and Justice's Interfaith Partners, enlisted our Interfaith Partners board and his family.

Reuniting the Children of Abraham was on its way!

Our next step was to find Metro Detroit teenagers from all three faiths willing to share personal stories about their experiences of navigating the complex boundaries around faith and ethnicity. Once we gathered a group, we were shocked to hear that every teen had been subjected to some form of religious, cultural or racial prejudice. Many already had developed a real fear of "the other."

We used the four-step process of reconciliation with these teens.

> **Step 1:** *Breaking bread together turned into sharing pizza.*

> **Step 2:** *As we began to listen with compassion, the young people shared deeply personal stories, including ways in which they have been hurt by racial or religious prejudice.*

> **Step 3:** *We reversed the narratives and listened as others retold the stories they had just heard. This deepened the experience and understanding of these stories as they were echoed through other voices.*

> **Step 4:** *The challenge to collaborate on creating something new became the development of a stage production, which we called, Reuniting the Children of Abraham.*

We realized that we were creating far more than a play. Once we were ready to begin performing the play itself, we extended the theatrical experience. After the final scripted lines, we would turn on the house lights and invite the audience to dialogue with the young actors about what we had just seen on stage. Those interactions were just as powerful as the play. Right away, we saw the potential to help communities not only in Michigan, but across the country and around the world.

Producing a play and then making that big leap toward additional performances took a whole lot of supportive friends! Victor Begg, co-chair of the Council of Islamic Organizations of Michigan, encouraged two of his children, Sofia Begg Latif and Yusuf Begg, to take part in the original workshop. My friend Julie Cummings was supportive from the very beginning. Then, Julie's family and my family were among five—including the Seligmans, Farbmans and Gershensons—who donated funds to produce *Reuniting the Children of Abraham*.

Eventually, entire cities got involved. The Kalamazoo-based Fetzer Foundation not only provided more funding for the project, but also brought a production to Kalamazoo and worked hard to bring many different groups together in their region of southwest Michigan.

Media professionals joined our ever-widening circle. The CBS television network produced a documentary about the project that aired nationwide, and we were featured in an hour-long special on Bridges TV, a national Muslim television network.

Reuniting the Children of Abraham now has friends all around the world. In 2006, we were asked to speak to more than 400 psychologists and psychotherapists from 70 countries at a "New Ways of Looking at Conflict" conference in Israel. We also met with Arab and Israeli high school students in Israel who participate in a similar project called Peace Child Israel. They were shocked to learn the Middle East conflict affected high school students in the U.S.

The project has opened many doors. Imam Mohammad Elahi gave me the honor of being the first Jewish woman to deliver a Ramadan sermon at a mosque in Michigan. Imam El Amin and I were keynote speakers at the 2006 National Humanities Conference in Louisville, Kentucky. In Atlanta, we spoke to more than 300 Jewish educators, most of whom had never met an imam. In 2007, I orchestrated an invitation for Victor Begg to address a national conference of rabbis—and Victor arranged for me to present *Reuniting the Children of Abraham* at the Islamic Society of North America, a gathering of more than 50,000 Muslims. In 2008, we were guests of the royal family in Amman, Jordan, where we presented the documentary in Arabic. That Arabic translation was supported by a gift of another friend: Mona Farouk.

Through all of this work and all of these travels, what interests me most is the question that started me on this long journey: Where can we find those individual sparks of light? Lasting transformation begins as one individual shares with another. I'm always looking for the change we can make in each life and each new friendship.

In 2016, I was attending an event at Imam Elahi's mosque, The Islamic House of Wisdom. I started chatting with Suzanne Bante, chair of the Interfaith Committee for Girl Scouts of Southeastern Michigan. Our friendship grew. In 2017, Suzanne was looking for a Jewish liaison and spoke to a Jewish focus group arranged by the Jewish Federation of Detroit.

Suzanne's talk to the group brought back numerous childhood memories. I was a Brownie and Girl Scout; my mother led our troop. Our pledge was to make the world a better place, which was the same as the Jewish belief of Tikkun Olam. I recalled the fun of earning so many badges that I had to get a second sash. That's why I agreed to serve as her liaison.

My latest chapter of interfaith engagement began with Suzanne's Girl Scouts. The girls and the leaders are incredible partners. In two short years, we have created ground-breaking programs, such as Experiencing a Jewish Seder, led by women. We have shared Jewish values, songs and Shabbat with 70 Catholic Girl Scouts at Holy Family Church in Rochester, Michigan. We have supported Hannah Richard's gold award for Relax Respect Respond, a program to create mutual understanding between police and community, especially during traffic stops. For January 26, 2020, we organized a *Reuniting the Children of the Abraham* day of discovery at the Detroit Institute of Arts—with a special, colorful patch so the girls can mark this special adventure.

In developing these programs, I have had some advantages—talents developed through a lifetime involved in marketing. I grew up around bright lights. My parents owned the famous Raven Gallery in Detroit—a meeting place for artists, musicians, writers and civic activists. In my twenties, I began a long career in fashion marketing, becoming the first woman vice president of fashion at the J.L. Hudson Co. and eventually was named Vice President of Fashion Merchandizing and Marketing for Federated, Allied department stores. At the chain's height, I identified the trends that would show up in more than 1,000 stores—including Hudson's in Michigan, Bloomingdale's in New York, Burdines in Florida and Bullock's in California. I've traveled widely, rubbing shoulders with influential people. I even dined in Monaco with Prince Rainier. So, I am able to call on friends from nearly every cultural background you can imagine.

However, this work over the last decade has taken more courage than anything else I've ever tried to accomplish. As a Jewish woman who cares about her Jewish community and about Israel, I had no idea my desire to bring Christians, Jews and Muslims together after Sept. 11, 2001, would be so controversial. That has not become any easier over the years! After the war between Israel and Hezbollah, keeping friendships on both sides of the divide took daring, stubborn determination and a clear vision that our hope for peace depends on maintaining all relationships.

That is where peace begins—in the relationships we form as we break bread together, share our stories with each other and begin to work together. That's when the light begins to shine.

That's why on January 26, 2020, I will be lighting 73 candles on my birthday cake at the Detroit Institute of Arts. I can't imagine a better gift than the opportunity to bring together over 200 Girl Scouts and their leaders from many different faith backgrounds as part of a new presentation of *Reuniting the Children of Abraham.* This new experience of our core ideas was developed in partnership with the Detroit Institute of Arts and Suzanne Bante's Interfaith Committee for Girl Scouts of Southeastern Michigan.

The day-long program is a special opportunity for the girls to take the lead in breaking down the longstanding barriers of stereotyping and intolerance across our communities. The vision for this program is to create what we are describing as a brave space, utilizing the arts to build bridges of understanding and communication.

The day includes a treasure hunt through the museum using a DIA web app created for the girls. At each stop, the girls will be asked to take a picture or write about what they are experiencing. It's an exciting new way to see both the beauty and differences in Islamic, Christian, Judaic, Hindu and African art. The program also includes participating in the original experience of Reuniting the Children of Abraham by viewing our documentary and engaging in discussion.

The Girl Scout Law is the focus of our day—that commitment to "make the world a better place." The experience will be interactive and inclusive. The girls will get to share aspects of their religion and culture that others may not know or understand. They'll also have the opportunity to present their ideas, hopes and dreams in ways that will foster peace in our community, region and the world.

This new book—and a special patch for participating in the *Reuniting the Children of Abraham* program at the Detroit Institute of Arts—represent my gifts to the Girl Scouts so they can create even more sparks. With these experiences behind them, I know they will light the way to a future with more love and understanding—a world with more hope and less hate.

That pathway of friendships, an ever-expanding community spreading from one person to another, is the key to lasting peace.

What do Judaism, Christianity and Islam share?

These religions are all monotheistic, meaning they teach there is only one God. Judaism is the oldest of the three. Islam is the newest. These religions are called the Abrahamic religions because all view Abraham as their patriarch and a major prophet. Shared scriptural foundations have created some similar practices and scriptural uses.

Source: *100 Questions & Answers about American Jews* by the Michigan State University School of Journalism.

What are the origins of these three religions?

According to the Hebrew Scriptures, Abraham formed the first covenant with God, and Moses received and presented to all the Jewish people the binding covenant of Torah or Jewish law, making God's law their own.

The Bible recounts that God told Abraham to go to Canaan. It is now known as Israel, named after Abraham's grandson. The land is often referred to as the Promised Land because of God's repeated promise to give the land to the descendants of Abraham. Judaism began about 4,000 years ago; it is the oldest of the three Abrahamic religions.

The primary language of the Jewish people and the Torah is Hebrew. The holiest texts in Judaism are the first five books of the Bible (Genesis, Exodus, Leviticus, Numbers and Deuteronomy), which Jews call the Torah and believe that God gave to Moses on Mount Sinai.

The Hebrew Scriptures, comprising the Torah, the prophets and the historical books called "the writings," were codified by Jewish religious scholars somewhere between 200 BCE and 200 CE. They are identical to books in the "Old Testament" Christians read; 100 CE is the date of the earliest Old Testament canon. At least one copy of the Torah in Hebrew is kept in every synagogue in the form of a hand-written parchment scroll. Jews read a particular, set portion of the Torah scroll every week in synagogue. The Talmud is a compendium of law and commentary on the Torah applying it to life in later and changed circumstances.

Christianity is founded on the life and teachings of Jesus Christ, a Jew. The religion is based on Jesus' teachings, sayings, healings, death and resurrection.

Christianity originated in the first century. The Bible recounts that Jesus was born in Bethlehem. Although the Western system for dating years is based on the birth of Jesus, historical evidence suggests that he was born around 4 BCE.

Jesus' native language was Aramaic, but the New Testament was written in Greek, the common language of the region. In addition to the Hebrew Scriptures, Christians rely on the New Testament, the name given to the Christian Scriptures that were written after the birth of Jesus. They consider these writings sacred texts.

Of the books that became part of the New Testament, the oldest are the letters of Paul, usually considered to have been written in the 40s and 50s of the first century. Other letters are thought to have been written over the next couple of decades. Of the four Gospels, Mark is considered the earliest at about 68-70 CE, while John is the latest at about 110. Acts is later than Luke (around 100) and Revelation was probably composed in the 90s.

Islam started with Adam and was transmitted by God through Prophets such as Adam, Abraham, Moses and Jesus; God finally preserved His message in the Quran though Muhammad, the last of the messengers. The word "Islam" means "submission" (to God's will) and "peace."

The language of the Quran is classical Arabic. Muhammad proclaimed that he first received Allah's (God in Arabic) revelations in a cave near Mecca, in present-day Saudi Arabia, beginning in 610 CE; he continued to receive new revelations until his death in 632 CE.

Muslims believe that the Quran is the actual word of God, revealed to Muhammad by God (Allah in Arabic). The Quran is not altered in any way since it was first compiled during Muhammad's life (570-632 CE). It has been written down in Arabic and many devout Muslims actually memorize the entire Quran. During the fasting month of Ramadan, men who have memorized the Quran and are skilled at reciting the text are called upon to recite the entire Quran at mosques across a series of evenings.

The only authoritative text of the Quran is in the original Arabic. Muslims regard "translations" of the Quran into other languages as paraphrases of the original. The Quran consists of 114 chapters (called "surahs"), which have names as well as numbers. They are arranged in the Quran according to their length, not in the order that Muhammed announced them or according to the chronology of stories that they tell.

Source: University of Michigan Arts of Citizenship Program, made possible in part by a grant from Michigan Humanities Council.

Who are some
of the important
early founders
and teachers in
these faiths?

Jews and Christians both use the word Patriarch in various ways. A Greek word, Patriarch means "chief or father of a family." Jews use the term to refer to three ancient founders. Christians also revere those founders and, especially in Eastern Orthodox branches of Christianity, the term is still used to refer to the leader of a particular branch of the Eastern church. Jews, Christians and Muslims all use the term prophet, as well, to describe humans who spoke with a special authority from God.

Jews use the word Patriarch to refer to three major figures:

- Abraham: Jewish tradition calls him the first monotheist, entering into a covenant with God that gave his descendants the Promised Land and committed them to worshipping God alone; according to the Hebrew Scriptures, he married Sarah, fathering Ishmael with his maidservant Hagar and Isaac with Sarah.

- Isaac: Abraham's second son; the Hebrew Scriptures tell that God asked Abraham to sacrifice Isaac as a test of Abraham's faith; he later married Rebecca and fathered Jacob and Esau.

- Jacob: Named "Israel" by an angel, which means "champion of God" and bore 12 sons, who would become the founders of the 12 tribes of Israel, or the Children of Israel.

Judaism also teaches that Moses is the most important prophet, teacher and lawgiver. According to Jewish teaching, God appeared to Moses and chose him to free the Children of Israel from Egyptian slavery and take them to the Promised Land. He led the Exodus of the Jewish people from Egypt and brought them to Mount Sinai. There, Jews believe, God gave Moses the Torah: the first five books of the Bible. Moses was said to have led the Jews in their 40 years' wandering in the desert of Sinai. He died just before the Children of Israel reached the Promised Land of Canaan, as a punishment for his disobedience to God.

In addition to Moses, there were other Jewish prophets who were essential in reinforcing the sacred covenant of restoring justice and peace to all people.

Because Christianity uses the Hebrew Bible as part of their Bible, Christians recognize the Jewish patriarchs and prophets. Much of the groundwork for Christianity comes from Judaism, including Jesus Himself, who was brought up in a traditional Jewish culture.

Jesus is also known as "Christ." "Christ" is a theological title meaning "anointed" or "the anointed one"; it is the Greek translation of the Hebrew Mashiach or "Messiah." Christians believe that Mary, the virgin mother of Jesus, conceived Jesus through the Holy Spirit. Jesus grew up to preach in Galilee and Judea with a message of repentance and forgiveness of sins through faith in the Kingdom of God. Jesus was executed by the Romans. He was crucified around 30 CE. Crucifixion was a long and painful process, and it was generally reserved only for criminals under Roman law.

Central to Christian belief is the idea that Jesus is both human and divine, and that God is experienced as a Holy Trinity: Father, Son and Holy Spirit. Jesus is the "Son" in the Holy Trinity. Christians believe that Jesus was resurrected from his grave three days after his execution and was seen by many people before he ascended into heaven. Christians also believe that Jesus' death was an act of atonement. The most common understanding is that by dying on the Cross, Jesus made it possible for those who believe in him to overcome the separation between themselves and God caused by sin and death.

The Christian New Testament recounts that Jesus had twelve core disciples or apostles to carry out his teachings. Most of the information about Jesus' life comes from the Gospels, the first four books of the New Testament. Two of the twelve disciples, Matthew and John, are named as authors. The other two named authors were Mark, a companion of the disciple Simon Peter, and Luke, a companion of Paul.

Paul, a Jew whose Hebrew name was Saul, had an enormous impact on the spread of Christianity. He never met Jesus and at first opposed Christians, but he had a vision of the resurrected Christ on the road to Damascus. He became an apostle of Christianity, traveling across the Roman empire to interpret and spread "the good news" of Jesus as the Christ. The first followers of Jesus were Jews. Paul was influential in making the church open to non-Jews as well.

For Muslims, the Prophet Muhammad is the final messenger, the recipient of the last of God's (Allah in Arabic) revelations preserved in its original form in the Quran. Muslims believe God's message is perfected in the Quran, the same divine message that existed since Adam. Abraham, Moses, Jesus and Mary are all mentioned in the Quran. Islam maintains that God communicated His message to all people in history. The prophets mentioned by name in the Quran are primarily those in the Bible.

The Prophet Muhammad was born 570 CE in Mecca, Arabia to a family of the Quraysh tribe. In his early life he earned the title "trustworthy (Al-Amin)" from pagan Arabs. At 40, Muhammad received his first revelation through Archangel Gabriel. After a gap of three years, the revelations continued for 20 more years. Muhammad and his few followers were persecuted for many years, preaching reform and monotheism to Meccan idolaters, and then were forced to migrate to Medina, where Muhammad established the first Islamic state. He was a preacher, statesman, soldier and exemplary family man before his death in 632. His sayings and traditions (Hadith and Sunnah) also are well preserved as the second source of Islamic faith after the Quran.

Source: University of Michigan Arts of Citizenship Program, made possible in part by a grant from Michigan Humanities Council.

What are some of the
distinctive beliefs
of these faiths?

Christianity:

- There is one God who reveals Himself in three "persons," described as Father, Son (Jesus Christ) and Holy Spirit. However, these three persons are regarded as a unity, sharing one substance.
- God has created the world distinct from Himself but is believed to be active within it as a Creator, Sustainer and Sanctifier.
- Belief in Jesus' divinity and in his teachings: No one can earn God's mercy or be righteous in His eyes, but one can know His infinite forgiveness and mercy through turning to Him; following the Sermon on the Mount and being a witness in daily life; belief in heaven.

Islam:

- Belief in one, omnipresent, almighty God who created the universe and all in it; belief in prophets, revelations, angels, the hereafter and divine decree.
- Islam encompasses all aspects of earthly life, governed by Islamic law (sharia) and organized around five pillars: belief in God and His messengers, daily prayers, charity, fasting, and pilgrimage (Hajj).
- Islam means total "submission" to God's will, achieving "peace" within.

Judaism:

- There is a single, all powerful God, who created the universe and everything in it.
- Jews are directed to be like God, to be Kadosh or sacred. Kedusha: seeking the sacred is central to Jewish beliefs. Judaism imagines a world in which each and every action has the potential for Kedusha.
- Each action or obligation that brings Kedusha into the world is called a mitzvah. Doing a mitzvah is the key that allows each person to experience the sacred. Judaism tends to be more focused on the actions of mitzvah than faith alone.
- The mitzvah of Tikkun Olam (to be God's hands here on earth and help repair the world) is central to Jewish belief.

Source: University of Michigan Arts of Citizenship Program, made possible in part by a grant from Michigan Humanities Council.

What beliefs are shared by these faiths?

The three religions share many teachings, including many specific texts that are almost identically worded in all three traditions. Among the shared beliefs:

- All human beings are created in the image of God.
- Monotheism, a belief in one God.
- Social justice and the concern for others.
- The pursuit of peace.

In addition, Judaism, Christianity and Islam all trace their roots back to Abraham, and believers all find inspiration in his relationship with God. In Genesis, God made a covenant with Abraham: "I shall make of you a great nation and all the families of the earth shall bless themselves by you." In the New Testament book of Galatians, the apostle Paul wrote, "Understand then that those who believe are children of Abraham. ... So those who have faith are blessed along with Abraham, the man of faith." The Quran, Surah 16, says, "Surely Abraham was an exemplar, obedient to Allah, upright, and he was not of the polytheists."

Source: University of Michigan Arts of Citizenship Program, made possible in part by a grant from Michigan Humanities Council.

How do the three
faiths relate the
sacrifice story?

God's call and Abraham's willingness to sacrifice a son represents one of the most powerful and important Abrahamic stories for all three faiths. Each tradition has interpreted the story in light of its own core values and concerns.

Jews read the akedah, the "binding" of Abraham's son Isaac, from Genesis each year on the High Holiday of Rosh Hashanah. In this account, Isaac asks his father as they approach Mount Moriah, "Behold the fire and the wood; but where is the lamb for a burnt-offering?"

Abraham answers, "God himself will provide the lamb for an offering." In this story, God does provide a ram. In Judaism, the harrowing incident underscores the covenant, the commitment that God and Abraham have made to each other, and a clear rejection of child sacrifice.

In the Quran, the story of the sacrifice does not name the son who accompanies Abraham to the place of sacrifice, but Islamic tradition holds him to be Ishmael. He is steadfast and forbearing, offering himself up willingly, an exemplar of submission to God's will. As in the Jewish tradition, God ultimately does not require Abraham to go through with this sacrifice. The Quran does not mention a ram as a substitute, but this remarkable spirit of sacrifice and obedience to God is celebrated in the annual Festival of Eid al-Adha, the Festival of Sacrifice, the culminating event of the Hajj. Muslims around the world join the pilgrims in Mecca to commemorate Eid al-Adha by attending religious services, visiting each other's homes, and sharing lamb as a symbol of Abraham's sacrifice.

Christians have viewed the story of Isaac on Mount Moriah as a forerunner of Jesus' death and resurrection. Jesus taught about God as fulfilling the covenant promise to create a new nation. After the Romans executed Jesus, Christians believe that God raised Jesus from the dead to establish a new covenant for all who believe. Just as Rosh Hashanah and Eid al-Adha commemorate the story, Good Friday and Easter evoke Abraham and Isaac in its remembrance of the death and resurrection.

Source: University of Michigan Arts of Citizenship Program, made possible in part by a grant from Michigan Humanities Council.

What is distinctive
about houses
of worship in
these faiths?

The Jewish house of worship is called a synagogue, or temple, which is actually a Greek translation of the Hebrew beit k'nesset: "place of assembly." The synagogue or temple is also known as a beit tefilah, a house of prayer. It is the place where Jews come together for community prayer services. The synagogue or temple is also a beit midrash, a house of study.

Probably the most important feature of the sanctuary is the Ark. The name "Ark" is an acronym of the Hebrew words "Aron Kodesh," which means "holy cabinet." The Ark is a cabinet or recession in the wall, which holds the Torah scrolls.

In Christianity, the Bible says that the church is actually the people, so Christians often use the term to refer to an individual congregation, an entire denomination within Christianity—or the entire body of Christians around the world. The term also refers to a Christian house of worship, a specific meeting place.

Altars occupy a prominent place in Roman Catholic, Orthodox, Anglican and other liturgical denominations. They are used to hold and to prepare the bread and wine used in the Eucharist. In Protestant churches, a table serves as the centerpiece of the Holy Communion service, a remembrance of Jesus' death and resurrection.

Some churches focus less on liturgy and more on the preaching of "the Word of God," which is why many churches are focused on the pulpit where "the Word" is preached. Christian churches can range from very elaborate to very plain.

Today, most synagogues and churches also have extensive seating areas where attendees can sit comfortably while a worship service unfolds. So, one of the biggest differences people see in a mosque is a lack of seating.

A mosque (masjid) is simply a place to pray. Mosques generally are simple buildings oriented so that people are facing Mecca as they form shoulder-to-shoulder lines for prayer. Some mosques are unadorned with plain walls; some are elaborately decorated.

Muslims have continued the Jewish tradition of not depicting people or images of God in their houses of worship, so decoration often takes the form of sacred inscriptions. Judaism teaches that representations of God's image are not allowed because God has no body. The Quran is clear that no one should make physical representations of either God or the Prophet, or even his companions, because no human being can conceive of God. However, Christians believe that it is helpful to display images of God, Jesus and Jesus' followers, because God became visible in the life of Jesus. Christians do not worship the statues, images or symbols, but venerate that which they represent.

Because mosques are spaces set aside for prayer, some mosques around the world are actually rooms located within other larger buildings. In the U.S., mosques have become more like churches in that they form the center of a religious community, but in the Islamic world, anyone can walk into any mosque and pray. Group prayers are similar to prayers that Muslims make while they are alone, but Muslims also teach that praying side by side with fellow humans regardless of race or class is beneficial to cultivating our humility.

Source: University of Michigan Arts of Citizenship Program, made possible in part by a grant from Michigan Humanities Council.

What is stereotyping?

Stereotyping is a preconceived and oversimplified notion about some aspect of reality, particularly people or social groups. Stereotypes are notoriously prone to spreading errors, exaggerations and bias. They foster prejudice.

People can be stereotyped for their ethnic group, race, national origin, sex, age, physical or mental ability, sexual orientation or social class—or any characteristic.

Religion is yet another category for which people can be stereotyped and discriminated against. Sometimes, religious groups can encourage stereotypes of others. In strengthening their own bonds within their faith community, members may view other religions with suspicion and fear.

Source: University of Michigan Arts of Citizenship Program, made possible in part by a grant from Michigan Humanities Council.

Have you ever faced stereotyping?

All the young people who have taken part in the *Children of Abraham* project say they are frustrated with the stereotyping of people based on their faith or cultural identity. We interviewed the project's original young authors about their experiences. Their responses show perplexity, dismay and anger, but they also offer optimistic and realistic suggestions as to how stereotypes can be curbed.

Read some of their comments. You may find your own experiences mirrored in their words.

> *"A cousin of mine was wearing Middle Eastern clothes and got on a plane. Someone made assumptions about him and shouted, 'He's got a bomb.' He was asked to leave the plane, even though there was no evidence of this. It was a shock, something you don't necessarily expect when you're living in America, the land of the free."*
>
> **Sofia**

> *"People assume that because I am a Zionist, I don't believe in a Palestinian state or that Palestinians have a right to statehood. I believe in a state for the Jews, but I want people to understand that you can support Israel without thinking Palestinians don't have rights."*
>
> **Miriam**

"The whole idea that biracial kids aren't really 'Black' is something that has been thrown in my face a lot. I'm not your modern definition of interracial, but I have light skin and know stupid people who believe that the lighter you are the less Black you are."

Nicole

"People think all Christians want to convert everyone and that we look down on everyone else's religion. They caricature our religion as negative and close-minded. It's true that it's a Christian's job to bring people to Christ and that we do believe it is the only way to salvation, but doesn't everyone want to share their religion if they think it will bring you peace?"

Jasmine

"I think stereotyping happens out of ignorance and non-tolerance of other humans. In the past, people always assumed I was anti-U.S. and non-patriotic, which is not true."

Abe

"When people don't understand one religion, have never met an individual of a certain religion, or never had any contact with a religion, they tend to believe stories about people of that religion more easily. As a Jew, I have sometimes been accused of being cheap or hoarding my money. Though this is partially true in my case—I like to think of myself as a person who doesn't waste money—it is definitely not true for many Jews that I have met."

Gal

"Where do stereotypes come from? I think stereotypes come from people's homes or from the media, such as 'Black people love fried chicken, are thugs, and are not very smart.' "

Adam

"We were talking about the Palestine-Israel issue, and a girl spoke about a rally where there was anti-Israeli talk and she thought: 'Are they bashing me? It never occurred to me that the rallies could be hurting someone like that so much. If I grow up opposing Israelis in the conflict, then I'm going to wind up opposing a lot of people who have good intentions but are put in that whole circle of people. Now I'm more careful about the things I get involved with because I don't know the impact it might have on different people."

Sofia

"I'm being honest. I inherited a lot of those old false myths, like: All Muslims are abusive because Allah told them to be; Jews killed Christians; Christians are crazy; and Hinduism is weird. Those were my beliefs, but with maturity comes growth. I decided to drop my impression of what was not true—and began to search for what was really is true."

Nicole

"I thought all Jews were very strict in every part of their religion. I thought they were really distant. Now I know that other Jewish teens are just like me. They like to have fun, go out and see movies. I also noticed that they were not really that different, except they had a different religion."

Adam

"At a conference, we were given an assignment to make a drawing that meant something to us. This girl drew an Israeli flag and put an 'X' through it. I got really offended, because I was standing right next to her. I wasn't able to express how I felt at the time, but we did end up talking afterwards. I think she was happy to hear my opinion, happy that I was able to tell her that some of her stereotypes about Israel just were not true. It's important for groups to talk to one another, to develop trust and friendships and understanding."

Miriam

"The Children of Abraham play addresses many assumptions and generalizations such as these that are harming our society today. We all have to learn to realize that just because someone is different from ourselves does not mean that that person is wrong, immoral or evil."

Gal

"With the Children of Abraham project, we visited two mosques, a synagogue, participated in a Catholic liturgy and went to a Baptist church. This was such a wow-factor that it made me want to learn more."

Nicole

"The only way to change this is to educate people, a long and difficult process. It's possible one person at a time—and sometimes one audience at a time."

Abe

Source: University of Michigan Arts of Citizenship Program, made possible in part by a grant from Michigan Humanities Council.

What did we learn in the four-step healing process?

We learned a lot when young people engaged in the four-step healing process!

Step 1: Breaking Bread. We invited Christian, Muslim and Jewish high school students to share pizza. We broke the taboo about speaking to those we see as different, strangers or enemies. They welcomed the experience.

Step 2: Listen with compassion. Lines of communication were established when participants shared their stories of being victims of hate and prejudice. They told their stories uninterrupted; no one was allowed to comment, judge or criticize. The teens felt they were being heard, some for the first time. Because they felt heard by the other, they perceived their thoughts and beliefs were recognized by the other. Because their sharing was not interrupted, they felt their thoughts and beliefs were respected.

Step 3: Be the other. The participants took turns role playing. First, they retold the stories of historical characters. Then, they began to retell and role play based on the experiences of the stories they had just heard from others in the group. By stepping into each other's shoes, they experienced new levels of understanding. Their thoughts and beliefs were validated, and they felt empathy for others' pain and circumstances. They saw that each person had different truths. They learned they did not have to change their personal truths—or agree with the others' truth—to validate the others' feelings and express empathy to the other. This is where the deep healing took place.

Step 4: Create something new together. We created a new collective story and an interactive talk-back after the presentation to help foster discussion. The teens felt it was crucial to show how they learned to express empathy, and validate each other's truths, without having to give up or change their own thoughts or beliefs. We began to hear things like: "You do not have to be wrong for me to be right." And, "We have different truths, but we can come together and create peace."

The program gave us the unique opportunity to tell the story of Abraham's children in a new light. We were able to symbolically heal the trans-generational wounds borne of the ancient sibling rivalry over a father's love and the demands for the fair share of their inheritance. We broke the barriers of fear, hate and intolerance. No matter how horrific the TV or newspaper stories, our hearts were opened to pursuing our dream. We felt we were making a difference. We were creating peace.

Source: Brenda Naomi Rosenberg

How can we ensure that our conversation is constructive and compassionate?

Remind participants: We are here to create—in the words of Martin Luther King Jr.—"the beloved community," where everyone is modeling and reinforcing respect, understanding, acceptance and empathy so we can create an atmosphere of safety and trust. Then follow these seven guidelines:

1. Put understanding others first, being heard second.
2. Be respectful. No insulting, judging, criticizing or blaming.
3. Only one person speaks at a time.
4. There are no "wrong" answers. Share honestly.
5. Share your own experiences. Try to speak in the first person, beginning each sentence with "I feel—" or "I believe—"
6. Share only once, until all participants have had a chance to share.
7. Open your mind and heart. Respect the thoughts, beliefs and feelings of others, especially when they are different than yours.

We suggest asking participants to read these seven guidelines at the beginning of our events and then to sign their name on the paper as a sign that they are committing to follow these principles.

Source: Brenda Naomi Rosenberg

What questions
can we ask to
spark discussion?

Here are some of the most effective questions we have asked over the years as groups have experienced *Reuniting the Children of Abraham*. They may sound simple, but they work!

What surprised you?
What moved you?
What troubled you?
How was your faith tradition represented?
What else would you like to share about your faith tradition?
What new questions do you have after this experience?
How will you continue the conversation you started today?

Source: Brenda Naomi Rosenberg

A Guided Meditation for an Interfaith Gathering

Guided meditations have been used at many of our interfaith gatherings to open up time and space for participants, minds and hearts to embrace the possibilities of our emerging community. Here is the text of one such meditation, which I call: "Like the Stars in the Sky—We Are Abraham's Vision."

Let yourself relax—and prepare to enjoy the wide expanse of the night sky.

Begin to close your eyes and let go of any tension—or expectations.

Notice any part of your body where you might be holding tension.

Take a deep breath in—then exhale. And, as you breath out, let those tense areas relax.

Feel yourself open.

Take another deep breath in—and, as you exhale, let yourself expand as you let go of any last tension.

Once again, breath in and allow yourself to relax as you breathe out.

Imagine that you are looking up at the night sky.

You are outside. The night is clear and calm. The stars are shining. The evening holds a quiet magic.

You are alone, but safe and calm in the quiet of the night.

A sense of awe fills your senses as you gaze on the expanse of sky.

Notice the brilliant diamond lights that blanket the heavens—stars that puncture the darkness.

Stars that extend into the infinite expanse.

Look over the whole sky and notice the beauty of the stars— from horizon to horizon.

See stars that sparkle—stars that remain constant—stars coming in and out of focus.

Let your eyes come to rest—seeing nothing but the limitless expanse.

Feel the expanse—sense the unlimited infinite that knows no boundaries—that goes on forever.

And now take another deep breath in—take this limitless expanse into yourself.

And now let go of your own limitations—expand into the night sky.

Live in the wonder—the mystery of the heavens.

And as you let go of your own limitations—connect with the awe—the expanse—that holds so much more than you can see with your eyes.

Connect with the sky—the sky which goes on without ending. You are a part of this limitless sky.

Allow yourself to fill—to expand—with the wonder of the moment—the miracle of the heavens.

Visualize yourself as a brilliant star—a sparking light.

In the story of Abraham, God takes Abraham outside of his tent to look at the sky and envision the future of his people. God compares the countless stars to Abraham's descendants who will be as numerous as the stars in the sky.

But perhaps it is not only an issue of numbers. Perhaps God wanted Abraham to go outside so he could appreciate the fact that each of his descendants would be like the stars—each one of us a world unto ourselves, yet by joining with others we become a display of beauty rivaling the expanse of the heavens.

Perhaps God took Abraham outside so that he could appreciate the fact that each of his children could dream great dreams—but should remain humble when realizing our small place in the universe.

Perhaps God took Abraham outside to teach him that sometimes we have to step out of our small tents, the place where we are comfortable to appreciate the great things we are capable of.

So see yourself as the brilliant star, capable of lighting up the universe—and move that radiant light from your heart to everyone in the room—send that light to your family, communities and to the entire world.

See that light bathe the world in light, love and peace.

When you are ready—allow yourself to return from this vision of the heavens.

As you open up your eyes and return to the room—know you are as limitless as the heavens.

You are a luminescent star—a light for peace.

Source: Brenda Naomi Rosenberg

How can we pray together for peace?

Here is a prayer we have used with Jews, Christians and Muslims gathered together:

We join together to pray for peace.

As the sons and daughters of Isaac and Ishmael, help us to turn away from the weapons of hatred—and establish Salaam, Shalom and Peace throughout our world.

Oh Source of Peace, give us the strength, and the love to replace fear with understanding.

Help us to see beauty in both our differences and what we have in common.

Give us the wisdom to make our world a joyful and holy place filled with all your children doing your will as one heart.

Dear God, give us the courage to be your messengers and never miss any opportunity to create peace.

Oh, Lord of Peace, we are gathered here as the children of Abraham, as one human family, bless our work. Bless us with Peace, Salaam, Shalom.

Source: Brenda Naomi Rosenberg

Where else can we turn to learn more about the connections between world religions?

100 Questions and Answers About American Jews with a Guide to Jewish Holidays. East Lansing: The Michigan State University School of Journalism, 2016.

100 Questions and Answers About Chaldean Americans, Their Religion, Language and Culture. East Lansing: The Michigan State University School of Journalism, 2019.

100 Questions and Answers About Muslim Americans with a Guide to Islamic Holidays. East Lansing: The Michigan State University School of Journalism, 2014.

Abraham: A Journey to the Heart of Three Faiths. Feiler, Bruce. New York: Harper Collins Publishers, Inc., 2004.

Blessed Are the Peacemakers. Buttry, Daniel L. Canton: Read the Spirit Books, 2011.

GodSigns. Farbman, Suzy. Canton: Read the Spirit Books, 2013.

Interfaith Heroes 2. Buttry, Daniel L. Canton: Read the Spirit Books, 2008.

Interfaith Heroes. Buttry, Daniel L. Canton: Read the Spirit Books, 2007.

Islam: A Short History. Armstrong, Karen. New York: Random House Inc., 2000.

Our Muslim Neighbors: Achieving the American Dream, An Immigrant's Memoir. Begg, Victor. Canton: Read the Spirit Books, 2019.

About the Author

Brenda Naomi Rosenberg describes herself in three words: Trendicator. Peacemaker. Ground-breaker.

From her background as a national trend-setter in fashion, design and marketing for major department stores, Brenda carried her creative passion into multicultural and inter-religious peacemaking after the terrorist attacks on Sept. 11, 2001. Through a wide array of initiatives, she established strategic partnerships and opened doors to men, women and youth from diverse backgrounds. Among her many efforts, she developed a cross-cultural approach to counseling and to designing educational conferences called the Tectonic Leadership program with Samia Moustapha Bahsoun, which is detailed in their book, *Harnessing the Power of Tension.*

Her goal has always been: "To make a more beautiful world by breaking barriers and re-framing relationships, utilizing creativity to actualize change."

Brenda's largest effort, which has blossomed into theatrical performances, workshops, small-group discussions and even a CBS network documentary is *Reuniting the Children of Abraham.* That popular multimedia program now is introduced to readers in this book, which includes inspiring stories, educational materials and small-group resources used in this program throughout the years.

Among Brenda's many other firsts:

First to break racial barriers at Saks Fifth Avenue by hiring black models in 1966 in Detroit.

First Jewish woman to deliver a sermon at a major mosque in the U.S.: The Islamic House of Wisdom in 2002.

First Jewish person and first woman to be honored by the Michigan Muslim Council.

First to conduct a week-long workshop connecting Christian, Muslim and Jewish students from four Michigan universities to learn how it is possible to have cool conversations on the hot topic of the Middle East—in partnership with Samia Moustapha Bahsoun in 2011.

In 2020, Brenda's message of hope to the world on the front page of her website, www.BrendaNaomiRosenberg.com is: "In a world marked by heightened tension between nations, groups, and individuals, the prospect of peace can seem elusive. But seeing the tension that is ripping us apart makes me more determined to build a better world."

www.ingramcontent.com/pod-product-compliance
Lightning Source LLC
Chambersburg PA
CBHW020214090426
42734CB00008B/1067

* 9 7 8 1 6 4 1 8 0 0 7 1 6 *